GOD IS EVERYWHERE

Brown Bear and Red Goose have two children, a gosling named Charity and a cub named John. They all believe in God.

God Is Everywhere
2012

ISBN-13: 978-1480037892

ISBN-10: 1480037893

God Is Everywhere

The Attributes of God for Children

Saturday morning Charity and John found Papa and Mama working in the garden. Their smiles said that they had thought of more questions to ask.

"Papa," said Charity, "If God has no body, then where is He?"

"What a good question!" said Papa.
"Let's see what the Bible says about it."

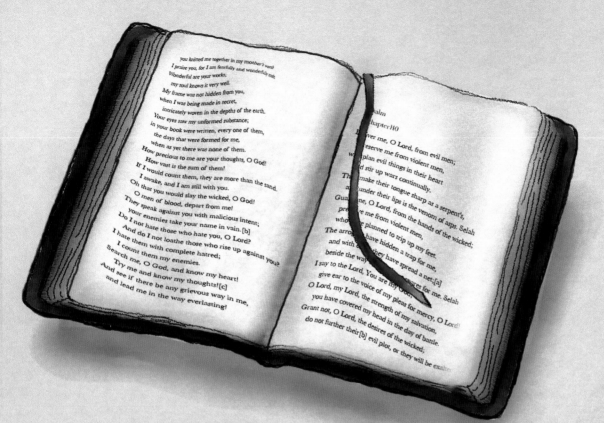

Papa took a Bible and read:

"I can never escape from your Spirit. I can never get away from your presence. If I go up to heaven, you are there! If I dwell across the farthest oceans, even there your hand will guide me, and your strength will support me" (Psalm 139.7–10).

"What does this tell us about where God is?" asked Papa.

"God is everywhere!" said John.

"That's right!" said Papa. "Since God doesn't have a body, He's not in just one place the way we are. He's everywhere!"

At that moment Mama came into the room carrying some glasses of cold milk and some freshly baked cookies.

"So is God in the cookies—and even in my glass of milk?" giggled John.

Papa laughed, too. "No," he said, "Since God doesn't have a body, He isn't really in any *place* at all.

"When we say God is everywhere, we mean that He knows what is happening everywhere in the whole world and that He is making things happen everywhere in the whole world."

"What does this teach us about God?" Mama asked.

"You can't run away from God," said Charity.

"That's right," Mama said.

"No matter where you go, God knows what you are doing, and He can help you there, too. What else?"

"You're never alone!" said John.

"Very good!" said Papa.

"No matter where you go, even if you fly to the moon, and nobody else is there, God is with you because He is everywhere. Aren't you glad about that?"

"Yeah!" shouted John, "'Cause someday I want to fly to the moon!"

Memory Verse:
"I can never escape from your Spirit. I can never get away from your presence." – Psalm 139:7

Books in the "What is God Like?" series

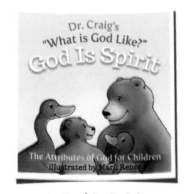

I. God is Spirit

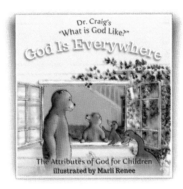

II. God is Everywhere

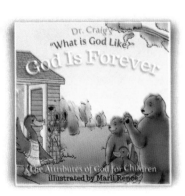

III. God is Forever

IV. God is Self-Sufficient

V. God is All-Knowing

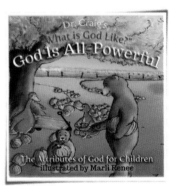

VI. God is All-Powerful

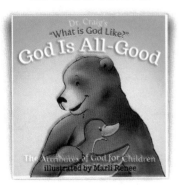

VII. God is All-Good

VIII. God is All-Loving

IX. God is Three Persons

X. The Greatness of God

N GUARD

Defending Your Faith with Reason and Precision

ILLIAM LANE CRAIG

BEST-SELLING AUTHOR OF REASONABLE FAITH

On Guard and *On Guard Study Guide*
are available at www.onguardbook.com

19437992R00015

Made in the USA
Lexington, KY
18 December 2012